D1496225

Invoking The Light

First published by PowerLight Enterprises 2005.
Designed, published and distributed in Australia.

You are welcome to visit our web site at
www.invokingthelight.com

Printed by McPherson's Printing Group.

National Library of Australia
Cataloguing-in-Publication data:
Reynolds, C. F.
Invoking The Light.
ISBN 0-646-45632-6.
1. Self-actualisation (Psychology).
2. Private revelations.
3. Self-perception. I. Title.
158.1

Invoking The Light

C. F. Reynolds

POWERLIGHT ENTERPRISES

DEDICATION

With gratitude, I dedicate this book to the
ever-present, sustaining and uplifting benevolence
of God the Source of The Light and my
Companion Light Beings, and my niece and
muse Renée for her dauntless encouragement.

Contents

Introduction

*I*n 1991, my spiritual journey began as I immersed myself in the study of meditation. A deeply spiritual experience, it provided a practical tool for self-actualisation. Since then, I have spent most of my time eliminating blocks I perceived to be standing in the way of achieving greater awareness. As my awareness grew, I removed many emotional blocks, and for a time, I felt I had made great progress. However, some blocks seemed to persist despite my best efforts, which included spiritual healing sessions, manifestation techniques and self-development books and courses—although beneficial, nothing had a lasting effect. In time, I manifested a successful business and lifestyle and a satisfying spiritual path, but my personal life continued to trouble me.

After the deaths of two beloved beings, my feline companion of 15 years and my beloved mother two months later, I entered a downward spiral of deep loneliness, loss and depression. Inconsolable, my grief consumed me. I found myself isolated from friends and family. In a fragile effort to block out the depression I visited a friend in Far North Queensland, where my spiritual journey ended and my Journey of Light began.

My friend and I took a fateful excursion to Mossman Gorge on Aboriginal land. The humidity washed over us as we walked along a bush-laden trail, winding our way down to the gorge. We stepped through a multitude of 'doors', created by trees growing on opposite sides of the trail, their lofty branches reaching toward each other to join across the top. Up ahead one white and one spotted piglet crossed our path. Amused, we laughed and thought it was a good omen. Our journey along the trail seemed magical.

At one point we stopped to rest. I closed my eyes to imbibe the natural energy pervading all around us. Suddenly, I noticed the colours in my mind's eye taking shape. They formed a circular image, containing a cross. Fascinated, I described the vision to my friend, who conjectured the image to be 'nature revealing itself'. After a few moments, the vision faded, and we continued our walk to the gorge. I thought nothing more of the mysterious vision as we enjoyed a tranquil day wading in the luminous waters of the gorge.

Two months later, I visited my niece in Germany and we travelled to France. Staying in the quaint town of Reims, we toured the stunningly beautiful Cathédrale Notre-Dame. We meandered through cavernous corridors, appearing to have no beginning and no end, adorned with sacred relics of faith and devotion. I stopped for a moment to close my eyes and immerse myself in the energy of that divine place. To my astonishment, the circular image reappeared. I began to think something spiritually significant might be linked to the image.

Shortly afterwards, my visions increased. Awakening in the middle of the night, I began to perceive an otherworldly dimension, only as outlines, again with my eyes closed. The most striking visions revealed an Egyptian landscape, replete with palm trees and a pyramid, and a cathedral with stunning stained-glass windows. In the latter vision, an angel walked onto the scene, bringing my mother into view, who had passed away only the day before. The angel seemed to be gently urging her to say 'hello', but she appeared hesitant. I sensed she was concerned about alarming me. I told the angel how beautiful I thought it looked, and it smiled at me, stretching out its magnificent wings!

When I returned home from my odyssey, I reasoned that all of these strange experiences were a consequence of spending far too much time alone, combined with deep emotional strain. Soon I returned to my usual routine, and for a while things seemed to resume normally.

One glorious summer day, after returning from a short jogging session, I thought I must have stared too long at the sun, since something blocked my vision. I shut my eyes and opened them. Directly in front of me, the circular vision reappeared for the third and final time, lasting for about one minute! Finally I took notice.

Although faded from view, the vision had etched its full impression on my mind. I used my computer to create an illustration of the circular image that haunted me. Like a beacon, it graces the cover of this book.

Necessity being the mother of invention, the next step of this mysterious process unfolded as a practical solution to negative experiences, plaguing my life for years and increasing with intensity in recent months. Once again, a jogging session would serve as an unlikely source of illumination.

As I jogged home one afternoon, a dog chased after me and nipped my heal. Agitated, I returned home and promptly proceeded to write a positive affirmation, convinced I had to purge myself of negative feelings in order to remove negative experiences. The affirmation I wrote that day did much more than simply vanquish the obstacles in my life. It transformed my consciousness and provided a spiritual quantum leap onto a powerful and accelerated path to illumination.

The moment I began reciting the affirmation, the negative experiences I had been having gradually ceased. However, for a short while, I noticed my negative thoughts and feelings increasing and conflicts still arose at times. Nonetheless, I persisted, driven by my new-found faith in the obvious power of the affirmation. The more I recited it, the more peaceful I felt. Conflicts gave way to harmony, and the negative thoughts and feelings eventually dissipated. With fewer difficulties, life became easy as my wellbeing heightened overall.

Encouraged, I repeated the affirmation continually. The mysterious visions increased as I received glimpses of a very skilfully hidden parallel dimension.

Additionally, I noticed frequent flashes of blue light and the distinctive scent of vanilla drifting in the air around me. Reciting the affirmation seemed to be elevating my frequency of light at an accelerated pace.

Inspired, I was driven to seek the underlying truth of these experiences. I sought a means to reveal this truth by way of a direct channel with the Divine Mind. In answer to my enquiries, I soon intuited a series of insights, revealing many truths as the Veil of Illusion shrouding my awareness in the physical world lifted. I embarked on a mission to share those truths with others in a very simple and straightfor-ward way. They grace the inside pages of this book.

Although *Invoking The Light* presents seemingly simple Light Truths, this revolutionary and dynamic spiritual practice, with its many revelations, may not be taken lightly. Although simplistic in form, it constitutes the most powerful spiritual path today, and at this phase of our human evolution, only the most courageous and dedicated spirit may embark upon it fully. Initially, you may face much opposition on an energetic level, but that opposition will soon weaken as limitless practical and spiritual rewards strengthen. The Light is love and truth in its purest form—when invoked, it will protect and empower you, always. In any case, *Invoking The Light* is flexible, assisting you throughout your Journey of Light, from the most practical to the highest way, leading to the ultimate state of human enlightenment.

Love, Grace, Blessings and Light,

C. F. Reynolds

PART I

FOUNDATION LIGHT TRUTHS

All You Need To Know Is The Light

*I*nvoking *The Light* challenges you to forget every-thing you know about a confusing array of New Age practices and psychological theories, requiring an enormous amount of effort to work, or often complicated religious practices, subject to so many different interpretations. Contrary to what everyone tells you, from your parents and friends to your therapist, consider for a moment the blissful possibility that you do not have to 'work on yourself' or 'resolve your issues'! You may recall the numerous occasions when you attended self-development courses or workshops, feeling optimistic and on top of the world, until something disappointing happened, sending you back to 'square one', or sought assistance to 'uncover the shadow within', only to encounter an elusive adversary.

Many of today's self-development books and courses, even an assortment of entertaining films, incorporate Light-based truths, but they are well hidden. Before you can imbibe the truths, you become so bogged down with distracting details—usually within volumes of verbiage, fast-paced adventures or heart-warming dramas—the truths end up buried in your subconscious mind like precious gems awaiting discovery. Originally, I had intended to take exactly the same approach but soon realised I had to take a chance and adopt a more direct approach to truly do justice to the truths I had uncovered.

From an early age, I believed in living life joyfully at every moment. In order to achieve such a sublime state, I used to think that positive intentions and clarity of focus were enough. Yet every time I set positive intentions, difficulties would inevitably emerge. I reasoned that negative experiences happened because I had to 'learn' in order to 'grow' spiritually. In truth, we need only live life FULLY AWARE. To become fully aware, all you need to know is The Light.

Whenever invoked, The Light does all the 'hard work' for you by dissolving blocks, while empowering and accelerating your positive intentions and illuminating your clarity of focus. Such a simple concept may seem extraordinary, but Divine Simplicity resides at the very heart of *Invoking The Light*. With just a few words, obstacles vanish as you illuminate your life.

We Project In the Physical World

The true nature of the physical world is quite simple. Reduced to the subatomic level, every person and every creature exits as pure energy. Any science student knows this fact. A divinely orchestrated, energetic matrix, the physical world actually constitutes a projection, tightly woven and real to the touch, made for and including us.

Then why do the physical world and our physical bodies seem so real, so solid? A Veil of Illusion enshrouds our physical world and every inhabitant. Often awakening in the middle of the night, I would perceive everything around me bathed in what appeared to be dot matrix and thumbprint-like patterns, which I had intuited to be the actual physical makeup of the Veil of Illusion. Not long after I first noticed these patterns, I watched a documentary on Albert Einstein and was amazed; towards the end of his life, he too perceived the world around him in the form of a subtle pattern. At the time, people assumed he was hallucinating because of his failing health. In deepening our focus, we perceive the less tangible and often subtle properties that make up the world around us. By invoking The Light, it is possible to perceive and momentarily lift the Veil of Illusion to reveal the truth of our existence.

Then what is the Veil of Illusion? The Veil of Illusion constitutes a kind of cosmic 'smoke and mirrors'. It blankets our awareness, so we may enter the physical world unaware, as projections. In this way, we may become aware of our true selves by transcending our projected awareness and embracing our Higher Selves, inevitably leading to our highest vision of ourselves. In truth, our Higher Selves are projections. Our pure essence emanates from God the Source of The Light.

Then why must we attain awareness? We seek to attain awareness through our physical projections. By living life fully aware in a pure state of connection and joy, we transcend the need to repeat our physical projections over and over again until we do.

To become aware, we must attain illumination. To attain illumination, we must know The Light.

Additionally, within the physical world, we project in the dream state. Dreams do not expose the psychological dramas of our subconscious mind in order to analyse them, as psychologists would have you believe. Primarily, they provide a way that we can transcend the limitations of the mundane physical world. The native Aboriginal people in Australia participate in 'the dreaming', and the Native American Indians induce dream states in order to experience visions. Just about every early civilisation denotes the importance of dreams. Many of us tend to discount ancient wisdom in favour of modern thought. Nonetheless such wisdom greatly benefits modern society.

By definition a projection is an impression—our souls, which drive our projections, constitute our true and timeless selves.

HIDDEN WORLDS PARALLEL OUR PHYSICAL WORLD

When I started invoking The Light, I began
to perceive an otherworldly dimension that had been
very skilfully hidden, revealing that three hidden
worlds parallel our physical world:

- Realm of The Light;

- Realm of Darkness; and

- Realm of Lost Souls.

The Realm of The Light is the domain of God
the Source of The Light and Light Beings, spiritual
projections of benevolent beings (usually archangels
and guardian angels, but such beings can assume any
benevolent symbolic form meaningful to the person
to whom they have been assigned). God the Source
of The Light assigns each of us Light Beings to
assist us in recognising The Light of Awareness.
Light Beings may not interfere with our choices
unless we permit them. They may assist and protect
us only through influence, either by way of other
people or telepathically.

The Realm of Darkness is the domain of the Source of Darkness and Dark Beings, spiritual projections of malevolent beings (usually arch demons and lower-level demons but such beings can assume any symbolic form meaningful to the person to whom they have been assigned, even a form disguised as benevolent*). The Source of Darkness assigns each of us Dark Beings to distract and confuse us, most commonly by way of 'negatives' or 'negative thought-forms', distorting our awareness and keeping us in the dark. Dark Beings may not interfere with our choices unless we permit them. They may undermine us only through influence, either by way of other people or telepathically.

Only through influence can Light Beings and Dark Beings affect us in the physical world, and NO ONE is immune to their influence.

The Realm of Lost Souls is a transition place for unaware souls that have passed from the physical world. Mirroring our world, this place can be

---

The only reliable way to distinguish a Light Being from a Dark Being or lost soul is to invoke The Light.

pleasant, or confusing, chaotic and even dangerous, therefore unstable. Being unaware, souls residing in this realm are lost, unable to detach themselves from their physical projections and find their way to The Light. Dark Beings exert a constant threat within this realm. Lost souls remain trapped until the light of a person in the physical world attracts them. A lost soul may be released when a person detects its presence within the light of his or her auric field and asks that it be taken to The Light. Lost souls can find The Light through us; therefore they must get our attention. Light Beings direct lost souls to The Light, but only at our request. Otherwise lost souls must wait until God the Source of The Light calls them. A lost soul's actions and behaviour determine the duration of its stint in this realm.

In basic terms, to experience itself, God the Creator projects as two distinct and separate sources— the Source of The Light and the Source of Darkness. Mirrored within our physical world, this separation of The Light and Darkness establishes the infrastructure that enables a support network of experience designed to bring about our enlightenment. Light Beings and souls/Higher Selves project from God the Source of The Light. The Source of Darkness recruits 'fallen' Light Beings to become Dark Beings by way of the ego and a false sense of personal power.

Witnessed by the Higher Self, the soul seeks to attain awareness through a physical projection by overcoming the challenges of the physical world enshrouded by the Veil of Illusion. Darkness blocks the soul's path to awareness through influence. A soul becomes a Light Being when it attains awareness and a Dark Being after living a projection mainly influenced by Darkness. Unaware souls must find their way out of, or be called from, the Realm of Lost Souls after each projection.

Once a soul becomes a Light Being, progression begins. However the potential always remains for a Light Being to turn to Darkness and a Dark Being to embrace The Light. To ascend from the depths of Darkness and attain awareness requires a soul to begin the process of physical projection over again.

A BATTLE FOR HUMAN SOULS REALLY EXISTS

This Light Truth may make New Age and mental health practitioners bristle, while relishing the opportunity to discount it. Modern thought maintains that people create evil influence rather than some invisible external source—another misconception concealing the truth courtesy of the Veil of Illusion.

Since time began this battle has raged on—a divine struggle between the legions of The Light and the forces of Darkness; Inner Light and the absence of The Light; Awareness and the lack of Awareness. Almost every creative work parallels this battle, often symbolised by a struggle with a seemingly invincible, deadly force combined with the hope of ones potential to rise above the struggle and achieve victory over adversity and seemingly impossible odds.

In truth, this battle takes place over each and every one of us, inside an auric dimension hidden yet emanating from the physical world. Additionally, this dimension enables Light Beings to enter our world and communicate their benevolent influence to assist us.

Dark Beings lurk about this dimension attempting to exert their malevolent influence aimed at undermining us, while promoting our ambivalence, doubt and eventual destruction. In this battle two sides reinforce two objectives—human illumination (Heaven on Earth) and human domination (Hell on Earth). The Veil of Illusion keeps this battle hidden, and we are not supposed to know about it. Invoking The Light is the only way to perceive and eventually resolve the battle.

The battle for human souls manifests in the physical world in so many ways, such as disagreements, conflicts, depravation, family derision and criminal acts. If enough fear builds it can lead to mental and physical illness, full-scale warfare and even natural disasters. Why? Whether by thought or action, reactions to fear in all of its forms have energy. Only the influence of Darkness provokes such reactions—herein lies the true tragedy of life. Instead of simply invoking The Light to vanquish Darkness before it can influence us, our reactions draw us into an ever-deepening emotional chasm, while the true culprit (Darkness) remains free to perpetuate its insidious influence.

A Power Play of Darkness Influences Us

To influence us, Darkness engages its 'battle strategy' based on the illusion of power by way of ego fulfilment and fear. This Power Play of Darkness elicits negative emotional responses.

Through the ego, Darkness promotes a false sense of self and power, while insisting if you eliminate the ego, you destroy your identity. This erroneous belief encourages us to mask our authenticity. Reinforced by the Veil of Illusion, the ego serves as a subtle and seductive mechanism to block awareness by raising and reinforcing a level of disbelief about anything not obvious to the physical senses or complying with the laws of the physical world. Darkness aims to keep everyone oblivious to the truth of our existence.

Darkness reinforces the belief that you need the ego to function in the physical world, maintaining it represents an essential part of our consciousness. Lacking awareness of the Higher Self, Darkness bases its existence on the ego, which identifies only with the mind and body of a physical projection. The physical form lacks substance until animated by a soul projecting to attain awareness. While the ego is empty and mortal, the soul is substantial and self-sustaining.

Our souls project in this physical world with individual 'chords' that have the potential to be 'played' by Darkness. When the Power Play of Darkness plays our chords, whether subtle or beneath the surface, we unconsciously react. Under such influence, our chords can elicit negative actions, such as anger, impatience, criticism, helplessness or self-loathing. Our chords orchestrate part of our projection and drive us in achieving awareness. After all, to know The Light we must recognise Darkness, which goes to great lengths to hide from our normal awareness. As you regularly invoke The Light you will stop reacting in a negative way in the event Darkness attempts to 'play you'.

When the Power Play of Darkness influences us and elicits a fearful response, it then plays upon those fears. Power plays often manifest as negative thought-forms, preoccupying us with worries involving fears that do not exist or fearful situations that may or may not happen. When the dreaded moment arrives and nothing happens, we wonder how we could have been so fearful in the first place! We could be sitting at our desks, working busily, or spending time with a loved one, when a fear suddenly arrives out of nowhere, popping into our heads just in time to ruin a blissful moment. It is the Power Play of Darkness 'playing us' and, unfortunately, working like a charm.

After you begin to invoke The Light, Darkness will try many ways to trick you into connecting with the ego. When you invoke The Light, you call forth the power of God the Source of The Light and His legions of Light Beings. As this power awakens within you, be sure to free yourself of any ego influence encouraged by Darkness. As projections, any sense of power we experience in the physical world comes from The Light. Even Light Beings project as vessels of power only, while Dark Beings promote the illusion of power.

True power only emanates from The Light, as evidenced by Light-based vehicles such as love, faith, trust, sanctity, clarity, compassion, courage, patience, forgiveness and humility. Only the illusion of power exists in Darkness, promoted by fear-based machinations such as confusion, doubt, anger, hatred, depravation, blame, conflict and revenge (however justified). Although Darkness exerts no real power over us, the Veil of Illusion serves as a kind of 'handicap', enabling Darkness to freely influence those possessing only normal awareness. Even a slightly higher than normal awareness dramatically reduces the effectiveness of such influence.

The true power of The Light always exposes and instantly dissolves Darkness, so we no longer need to react to the illusionary, fear-based influences it exerts. The Light empowers us, while Darkness overpowers us—if we allow it. Only by invoking The Light may we quash the power plays engaged by Darkness. Over the ages, many techniques have been applied to remove Darkness, but only The Light literally dissolves it. Otherwise, it disperses and moves on or lies dormant until it influences another person. Whenever you sense lost souls, negatives or negative thought-forms, always invoke The Light.

To illustrate its insidiousness, Darkness pervades religious institutions by promoting fear-based or ego interpretations of Light-based truths. All such skewed belief systems promote a general mistrust of anything other than 'tried and true' mainstream religious beliefs—even though, in truth, no belief is immune from the subtle influence of Darkness. Even New Age concepts either thoroughly discount or entirely ignore the existence of evil influence. Although many such practices offer beneficial alternatives to traditional religious practices and opportunities for self-actualisation, some can be spurious.

Should we remain reluctant to raise our awareness and allow Darkness to persist unabated, it will gain a foothold and, at the very least, divert us from reaching our highest potential and, at worst, threaten the delicate energetic balance of the physical world.

The Light offers a way to completely dissolve the influence of Darkness, while empowering us in attaining The Light of Awareness. Finally, *Invoking The Light* offers the most practical and powerful arsenal against Darkness.

In order to truly benefit from invoking The Light, we must acknowledge the existence of God the Source of The Light, the Higher Self as the witness of the soul's Divine Strategic Plan (as described in our next Light Truth) and the insidious influence of Darkness and its exhaustive power plays.

We prefer to discount the presence of evil or anything else we cannot readily perceive with our physical senses. Although in a physical world enshrouded by a Veil of Illusion we do not always know, we must believe, thereby adopting an attitude of trust, driven by faith, for our greatest good.

We Follow a Divine Strategic Plan

A Divine Strategic Plan determines everything we do in the physical world. We develop the plan with God the Source of The Light and complete all of the decision-making BEFORE we project. Once we form our projections, we simply allow the plan to unfold. For this reason, 'free will' in the physical world is an illusion. The plan unfolds throughout every moment of our lives, providing a road map for every choice we make, and at a deep level we know every aspect of our plan. This hidden knowing occasionally surfaces as psychic or deja vu experiences and the feeling that sometimes we seem to operate on autopilot.

To varying degrees, The Light and Darkness influences the plan. Our state of awareness at the time we develop the plan governs our choices. Always, under the benevolent influence of The Light, we are free to choose our path to enlightenment, even if we allow our path to be influenced by Darkness. For example, a soul with little or no awareness may inadvertently make a choice influenced by Darkness that, at first glance, appears to be easier than the choices presented by The Light. True wisdom resides in the saying describing 'a smooth road to hell and a rocky road to heaven'!

As souls, our ultimate goal is to progress, starting with attaining awareness through a physical projection. Projecting as the soul, the Higher Self witnesses the Divine Strategic Plan unfolding, while driving the physical projection. If the soul attains awareness, it immediately progresses to Light Being and at the end of its projection enters the Realm of The Light. Although progression from this point no longer requires a physical projection, Light Beings can re-enter the physical world as required.

To achieve specific objectives by way of a more direct influence, Light Beings can project in the physical world (so can Dark Beings). Projected Light Beings benefit others through benevolence and inspiration. Such individuals tend to work behind the scenes anonymously, with no desire to attract notoriety. Conversely, Projected Dark Beings exhibit extreme antisocial behaviour and show no remorse or regret for their actions, ranging from a general disregard for the feelings of others to heartless criminal acts. If you ever find yourself asking, 'How can anyone do something so evil?' it is very likely you are commenting on the actions of a Dark Being. Of course, such actions are not always obviously 'evil'. Many apply a subtle influence to distract us and sabotage our enlightenment.

On a Journey of Light, recognising the influence of Dark Beings in our lives, projected or otherwise, is important. If you detect negative people or circumstances, silently invoke The Light around yourself, and allow The Light to envelop all areas of your life. Dark Beings, or anyone under their seductive, charismatic or dangerous influence, will be unable to remain in your presence, since they cannot tolerate anyone who invokes The Light.

Once you begin invoking The Light, take note of the people that suddenly drop out of your life, as well as the positive, Light-based people and situations that enter your life.

YOUR SENSES WILL HEIGHTEN

While regularly invoking The Light, you may begin to see blue flashes of light appearing around you and others. Additionally, you may sense the aroma of vanilla, cookies or roses drifting in the air around you or in some rooms of your abode. Such signs serve as evidence that your frequency of light is elevating, and you are able to detect the presence of Light Beings.

Alternatively, Dark Beings prefer to remain unseen, although by invoking The Light you can perceive them in a variety of ways—much to their surprise. The most obvious way to detect Dark Beings is through unpleasant feelings such as confusion, doubt, discomfort or anger. As you become more aware, such feelings serve as warning signs of the influence of Darkness by way of the Power Play of Darkness. Whenever we experience negative feelings or detect negative thought-forms, we simply invoke The Light and they vanish immediately.

Invoking The Light enables you to lift the Veil of Illusion, which may trigger your Higher Vision—the vision of the Higher Self. Generally, such vision occurs as you awaken in the middle of the night. With your eyes closed, the inside of your eyelids become a kind of projection screen. Higher Vision alerts us to the presence of Darkness. Usually, the easiest visions to perceive are that of lost souls, followed by Dark Beings and Light Beings.

Through Higher Vision, invoking The Light may appear in symbolic form as an outline of the sun, which bears the likeness of God the Source of The Light, or as a massive whirlwind-like motion, sweeping up and taking away, in a flash, all manifestations of Darkness that may be present. Since we are invoking a power beyond our imagining, such visions serve as representations of recognisable images with which we may easily identify. As the most powerful energy source in our galaxy, the sun serves as an appropriate symbol to help us recognise the pervading bliss of God the Source of The Light. Additionally, the symbolic whirlwind effect serves as an apt representation of the incredible power of invoking The Light in removing Darkness from our lives when requested.

Since I was very young, I have been able to perceive lost souls. Even with the smallest amount of awareness they are easy to detect because they are the most attached to our physical world and their former projections. Living an illusionary existence, lost souls often masquerade in a symbolic form to attract our attention. Some lost souls may even appear quite indignant as you ask your Companion Light Beings to gently take them away!

After I began invoking The Light, I awoke one night to a vision of a battle raging over me between angels and demons! In case they were lost souls I tried to move them on to The Light but the battle raged on. When the vision faded, I intuited the reason why they were fighting. Apparently, the angels were protecting me against demons attempting to mobilise their forces in order to stop me from invoking The Light!

Two nights later another vision etched a power-ful impression on my mind. It revealed an imposing figure with outstretched, bat-like wings and a three-pointed head. Its stance appeared non-threatening and more curious, as if to say 'I am on to you' as it sat opposite my view with fingers loosely interlaced. I asked that it be moved on to The Light and watched as my Companion Light Beings came into view. Instead, they stood by as the figure slightly tilt-ed its head in their direction, giving them a side-glance as if to say 'I will let myself out, thank you'! Once the scene faded from view, I opened my eyes and knew that I had nothing to fear. I realised the significance of the vision and of the truths I was uncovering, as the mysterious process initiated by invoking The Light continued to unfold.

Additionally, expect your sense of smell to heighten in sensitivity. As I regularly invoked The Light, I began to detect the lovely scent of vanilla drifting in the air around me and often in corners of a room. I intuited my ability to detect the mysterious scent as an indication that my frequency of light had elevated, and I was experiencing a close connection with my Companion Light Beings. Shortly afterwards, my niece visited me, and we regularly invoked The Light together. Soon she began detecting the vanilla scent! A short time later, I began to detect another distinctive scent: a lot like chilled dirt or smoke. I determined this scent to serve as a warning alerting me to the presence of Dark Beings trying to get close enough to exert an influence. Being able to detect both Light Beings and Dark Beings in such a way was a revelation. While writing this book, I found myself under constant threat from Dark Beings eager to stop me from revealing these Light Truths; faced with the true power of The Light, eventually they relented. Still I had to stay on guard.

Such heightened senses assist us in detecting the benevolent presence of Companion Light Beings, as an affirming sign of comfort and support, and as a warning in the case of Dark Beings, commonly present in the form of negatives and negative thought-forms, before they may exert any kind of influence. By invoking The Light, Dark Beings instantly dissolve.

Always monitor any negative thoughts or feelings you may experience. The moment they occur, invoke The Light—think of them as just another form of early warning sign. In this way, negative experiences will begin to diminish and eventually stop altogether. God the Source of The Light loves effort—only a small effort reaps extraordinary rewards.

WE HAVE A DIVINE LIFE PURPOSE

What do you consider to be your life purpose? Does your purpose in life involve the work you perform, the family you love and care for and the friendships you nurture? Although important, these earthly life experiences constitute only a portion of your life purpose.

In truth, everyone has a Divine Life Purpose, comprising two basic stages. These stages may be described as mundane and highest, earthly and heavenly or ordinary and extraordinary. Most of us only choose to experience the first stage. It takes a spiritual quantum leap to transcend an ordinary life purpose to embrace the challenge of an extraordinary Divine Life Purpose.

A Divine Life Purpose provides a foundation enabling us to raise the frequency of light in all of our activities. Examples of major Divine Life Purpose types include:

- To Initiate (igniting self awareness)

- To Change (altering the course of history)

- To Protect (vanquishing Darkness)

- To Heal (spiritual, emotional and physical)

- To Support (uplifting and helping others)

- To Empathise (taking on and vanquishing suffering)

- To Sacrifice (inspiring others by living a long state of suffering or a short, tragic life)

Invoking The Light activates the second stage of your Divine Life Purpose. In doing so, regardless of how it may manifest, The Light will empower your purpose in life within an ever-increasing state of sublime awareness. We expend so much of our energy coping with the Power Play of Darkness and all of the subtle ways it influences us. Imagine the heights you will be free to reach as The Light vanquishes all fear from your life and the lives of those you love!

DISTRACTIONS KEEP US IN THE DARK

Sitting in front of the television one night, while I skipped through the channels, as usual, suddenly a thought struck me—as a powerful medium of influence, television serves to desensitise and shape points of view. In a highly suggestive and subliminal way, it triggers excessive consumerism and keeps viewers subdued. I recalled a moment in my childhood when I sat transfixed as the ads appeared and then became disinterested when the show returned. Suddenly the reason why I avoided many television shows and advertisements occurred to me. In truth, television keeps us preoccupied and therefore has the potential to distract us, becoming a potentially fertile playground for the Power Play of Darkness.

Television joins many preoccupations that potentially distract us from actualising The Light of Awareness. Even positive experiences, if allowed to overwhelm us, create the distractions needed to keep us in the dark. Such distractions can develop into obsessive preoccupations over enhancing ones appearance, engaging in hobbies or sporting activities or worshipping celebrities to name only a few. Certainly a healthy level of interest in such pastimes adds to the overall enjoyment of life. They become distractions when we allow such activities to take over our lives and block our awareness. If we look deeply enough, we discover that all obsessions involve a fear of some kind.

Clearly, most advertising, television shows and films, and particularly newscasts, play upon our fears. To illustrate this point, as I watched the news one evening, I was pleased that the last story had an uplifting theme. However, I was soon disappointed when the news wrapped up with gruesome images of a shark attack. Of course, television and film have the potential to entertain, amuse and motivate us. One of my favourite pastimes involves curling up on the couch and watching a good psychological thriller. By regularly invoking The Light, we reject all forms of influence promoted by Darkness, encouraging producers to take a more uplifting approach.

Even some parts of holy texts play upon our fears. Although divinely inspired, they were written at a time when fear prevailed, thereby blocking much of the meaningful interpretation of those messages. Darkness always deems it necessary to play upon our fears in order to awaken them. Inadvertently, many religions promote such an approach, yet their legions of faithful followers remain subdued and no closer to actualising The Light of Awareness. Notably, after I started invoking The Light, I actually began to enjoy reading the Bible again, as I perceived the higher messages in a new light.

In a world without awareness, Darkness freely and secretly exerts its subtle yet powerful influence in so many ways.

In Dreams We Transcend the Physical World

Dreams provide a way for us to transcend the limitations of the mundane physical world. In the dream state, our souls travel to other dimensions, momentarily freeing ourselves from our slumbering projections. The souls of people we know, both living and those who have passed, symbolically project to us in our dreams. Additionally, lost souls project in our dreams in order for us to move them on. If our Divine Life Purpose is 'to protect', we can enter the Realm of Lost Souls by way of our dreams to undermine negatives that may be tormenting lost souls and show both negatives and lost souls the way to The Light.

Dreams enable us to recognise fears in order to dissolve them. When we experience fearful dreams, we expose the fears influenced by Darkness in order to purge them. Projecting as nightmares, our fears take on a tangible and symbolic form with which we may grapple. In this way dreams indicate our level of awareness. With little or no awareness, we allow fears to take control in our dreams. Invoking The Light immediately renders fear impotent, empowering us to take control when fears manifest in our dreams. To illustrate this point, in a recurrent dream a dark figure projecting as someone I once knew very well stalked me. Gradually, the dream evolved: I started out running for my life then fearlessly confronting the dark figure and eventually grabbing hold of its collar, exposing the truth and uncovering the illusion. The recurrent dream abruptly ended.

Ultimately, dreams serve as a tool of The Light, aiding our spiritual transformation by helping us to clarify our Divine Life Purpose and reveal hidden truths that guide us as our Divine Strategic Plan unfolds. Keeping a journal at your bedside becomes an essential part of your Journey of Light and an effective vehicle in documenting the valuable insights revealed in your dreams.

INVOKING THE LIGHT IS SIMPLE YET POWERFUL

Imagine yourself as a participant in an advanced driver-training course. If your vehicle begins to skid, you are already out of control; therefore 'turning into' the skid will only make things worse. The idea is to engage the skills that will prevent the skid from happening in the first place. By invoking The Light you diffuse your reaction to fear (the skid) before you slide out of control. Fear becomes real only when we react to it. We must react in order to animate fear.

As an example of how brilliantly invoking The Light has worked for me, I live on one of the busiest street corners in Melbourne, Australia. For some time after moving in, I was bombarded day and night by the sounds of traffic, screeching tires and grinding breaks, thumping base from car stereos, and the frequent deafening sound of emergency sirens. Neighbours on almost every side played music at 'disco velocity' every weekend and sometimes during the weekdays. At night, two nightclubs sat on opposite corners, playing blaring music and attracting drunk, loud and aggressive patrons. One of the nightclubs hosted a 'graffiti night', attracting under-age drinkers—the next day I found graffiti on my walls emblazoned with paint provided courtesy of the nightclub! Other features of the area included a nearby methadone clinic attracting drug users, and prostitutes walked the streets day and night screaming at each other in the wee hours of the morning. One night a blood-chilling crash jolted me awake. I found out the next day that a car had run into a pole on the opposite corner of the street and burst into flames—bouquets of flowers hung all around the charred area. I witnessed several fender benders and a pedestrian knocked down by a car in the middle of the street! During the six months prior to intuiting the invocation, I had experienced several fender benders of my own.

When I first began invoking The Light, I was stunned by the power working through me. Initially, I began reciting the invocation every time I experienced negative people or situations. One night, a group of loud and aggressive young men loitered near my home. I invoked The Light, focusing on removing negatives and, as if by magic, they walked away! Within a short time, incidents involving my car stopped, quiet neighbours moved in all around me, one of the nightclubs closed down, and most of the time I did not even notice the traffic. Relatively speaking, the area became quite peaceful. However, I had noticed that sometimes if I would leave the area for an extended period, Darkness would return, as evidenced by negative situations. When this happened, I simply invoked The Light within myself and the area, and peace returned quickly.

We cannot vanquish Darkness completely from the physical world. It makes up part of a mysterious and intricate tapestry of experience designed to bring about our enlightenment. However, by frequently invoking The Light around yourself, your home and your neighbourhood, you can build your frequency of The Light to create a protective Energy Bubble of The Light. Eventually, you will invoke The Light at an unconscious level, as evidenced by the absence of fear in your life and an overall sense of emotional balance. Invoking The Light whenever you may encounter negative feelings, people or situations further builds upon this foundation. Once you begin invoking The Light you will significantly improve all aspects of your life, as well as attract Light-based people, situations and opportunities. Where The Light is present, Darkness weakens and dissolves, obstacles vanish and healing takes place at every level as you renew your life.

While invoking The Light, should any delays or negative experiences occur, accept them as Divine Signs. I can recall many occasions when a delay actually helped to avert a potentially awkward, unpleasant or even harmful situation, or guided me in the ideal direction in achieving my personal goals. Importantly, negative experiences provide valuable insights that hold clues to unravelling the intricate process of enlightenment. Under the benevolent influence of The Light, all experiences help guide us in playing out every nuance of our Divine Strategic Plan and Life Purpose. However, by regularly invoking

The Light, even Divine Signs eventually cease to serve a purpose in your life, since The Light hones your inner knowing. Additionally, The Light may draw such situations to you because they involve someone who needs the benevolent power of The Light. Seemingly negative experiences must never be taken personally. When invoking The Light all experiences become part of a Divine Denouement.

Importantly, avoid the influence of the ego when reciting the invocation. Always invoke The Light within yourself. However, if you feel the need to focus on a particular situation, additionally invoke The Light around others or activities but only with the intention of removing negatives and negative thought-forms that may be blocking you. In any case, you will be unable to impose any kind of will on others by invoking The Light because it vanquishes the ego whenever invoked. Therefore, the best outcome always manifests, often in ways that you may not have considered and always for your greatest good. Invoking The Light offers a powerful tool to illuminate your life.

To effectively invoke The Light, recite the invocation aloud or silently, while imagining yourself as a Vessel of The Light, filled with the radiance of the sun until your physical body transforms into The Light, then radiates outward. Always imbue meaning into your invocation.

Initially, fearful or ego-based thoughts or feelings may seem to increase. Do not ignore them. The moment they occur, invoke The Light as a kind of 'spring cleaning'. Continuing to regularly invoke The Light will eventually enable you to BECOME The Light—the sublime state of living life fully aware. At that point, you will recognise and dissolve Darkness before its power plays can influence you.

Invoking The Light is simple, yet so powerful. The invocation appears on the next page...

I invoke God's Grace,

which fills me

with Light.

Light dissolves all

Darkness.

PART II

LIVING THE LIGHT

WELCOMING YOUR COMPANION LIGHT BEINGS

Your Companion Light Beings assist you when needed to recognise the Power Play of Darkness and its many subtle manifestations before it may exert any influence. Devoted to your illumination, Companion Light Beings give you all the love, support, protection and inspiration you need to become The Light. Literally, they represent your soul mates throughout your Journey of Light.

Generally, whenever we invoke The Light, our Companion Light Beings:

- protect us and remove negatives and negative thought-forms to be dissolved into The Light; and

- guide and support us, while taking the lost souls we encounter to The Light.

To request the guidance of your Companion Light Beings most effectively, express your gratitude rather than asking, because your needs are met the moment you do. Commonly referred to as guardian angels and spirit guides, your Companion Light Beings provide their benevolent guidance and protection and serve as Vessels of The Light. Whenever we invoke The Light, we call forth the benevolent all-pervading power of The Light to channel through our Companion Light Beings to us, strengthening our clarity of focus and enabling The Light to do all the work for us in dissolving the influence of Darkness, thereby freeing us to live our lives more effectively.

As you regularly invoke The Light, your intuitive skills will heighten substantially, enabling you to connect with your Companion Light Beings. Initially, you may wish to use Light-based vehicles such as a deck of inspirational cards. Just be sure to invoke The Light each time you consult your Companion Light Beings, just in case any Dark Beings are lurking about—they love nothing more than to confuse you. Just remember—when in doubt, invoke The Light!

Your Companion Light Beings communicate to you in unlimited ways. They may speak to you in the next billboard you see or in a conversation you overhear while shopping. As you invoke The Light, your perception and psychic and intuitive abilities will grow at a rapid pace. Generally, you will gain a renewed perspective on your perception of mundane reality, as miracles become a natural everyday occurrence.

To acknowledge and welcome the benevolent support of your Companion Light Beings, recite the following invocation three times:

I invoke God's Grace, which fills me with Light. Light dissolves all Darkness, as I acknowledge and welcome with great love, respect and gratitude the benevolent guidance and protection of my Companion Light Beings:

Love, Grace, Blessings and Light to all.

Dissolving 'Assigned' Dark Beings and Persistent Negative Beliefs

To be freed from the influence of Darkness, your first task will be to dissolve your 'Assigned' Dark Being. On a few occasions, I noticed that when I was constantly invoking The Light, I still encountered a negative experience, although I barely reacted. I promptly intuited that I needed to dissolve my Assigned Dark Being.

Once you begin invoking The Light to dissolve all Darkness, your Assigned Dark Being manages to hang on, being the most difficult form of Darkness to dissolve. Like your Companion Light Beings, your Assigned Dark Being has been with you since the beginning of your projection and knows you well. It knows when you may invoke The Light and hides in the Realm of Darkness until the 'coast is clear'. It remains steadfastly in your presence, until you invoke The Light to dissolve it.

In consciously acknowledging its existence, you release Darkness in all of its forms from your life by dissolving it into The Light. Remember, Darkness supports our refusal to believe in its existence, while maintaining that NO knowledge has power. Aside from the obvious benefits, invoking the benevolence of The Light to dissolve your Assigned Dark Being presents it with an opportunity for redemption.

To dissolve your Assigned Dark Being, first welcome the assistance of your Companion Light Beings and acknowledge with gratitude the part inadvertently played by your Assigned Dark Being so far in your enlightenment. Then, recite the following invocation three times:

I invoke God's Grace, which fills me with Light. Light dissolves all Darkness and any and all Dark Beings assigned to me, or otherwise present in my life, from all time, space and dimensions and never to return:

Love, Grace, Blessings and Light to all.

Thank you God the Source of The Light and my Companion Light Beings for the benevolent gift of The Light.

This invocation applies a very specific focus for your intention, which is needed in such an instance. Although counterproductive, Assigned Dark Beings play an indirect role in supporting our ultimate goal of attaining The Light of Awareness.

Additionally, you can tailor this ritual with the aim of dissolving any fears persistently manifesting as negative habits, attitudes or beliefs. At the very least, such manifestations can hold us back from achieving our highest potential. Again, a very specific focus and intention help eliminate what can involve deeply entrenched fears. An example of an invocation to dissolve a specific negative belief may be recited as follows, three times:

I invoke God's Grace, which fills me with Light. Light dissolves all Darkness and my erroneous belief that I am (a failure at love) from all time, space and dimensions and never to return:

Love, Grace, Blessings and Light to all.

Thank you God the Source of The Light and my Companion Light Beings for the benevolent gift of The Light.

CREATING A SACRED SPACE

Creating a sacred space will help you transform your abode into a supportive foundation for every aspect of your daily life and an uplifting, safe and nurturing atmosphere for setting up a meditation practice, if you choose. The following guidelines will help you imbibe The Light throughout your home.

First, clear your abode of any negatives and negative thought-forms by creating a supportive and nurturing Energy Bubble of The Light, filling your home and extending outward, enveloping you, your home and your immediate neighbourhood. You may have a preferred clearing method. If not, some suggestions include ringing a bell, scattering salt, or lighting a smudge stick or several sticks of your favourite incense and wafting the smoke with a large feather.

Before beginning your sacred clearing ritual, welcome the benevolent presence of your Companion Light Beings and express gratitude for their guidance and protection. As you clear your abode, continuously invoke The Light, as follows, remembering cabinets, closets and the corners of all the rooms:

I invoke God's Grace, which fills me and my home and neighbourhood with Light. Light dissolves all Darkness, enveloping me and my home and all that I have and love with a Divine Barrier Shield Energy Bubble of Love, Grace, Blessings and Light:

Love, Grace, Blessings and Light to all.

After you have cleared your entire home, you may wish to select a sacred meditation space. Start by walking around your home to locate a quiet place away from foot traffic where you may meditate in complete privacy. Consider this area your personal sacred space. Ideally, your meditation space should occupy a room other than your bedroom; if your abode is small or if you share it with others, select a corner of your bedroom and section off the space using a room divider, such as a Japanese screen.

Depending on your preferences, you may wish to place the following items in and around your sacred meditation space:

- Pillows and a woollen cloth or lambskin on the floor or on a comfortable chair.

- A votive candle to represent The Light (be sure you safely contain it within an appropriate holder).

- Symbols of healing, tranquillity or devotion most meaningful to you, such as crystals, incense, chimes, fresh flowers or photographs.

Adopt a regular clearing routine to suit your personal circumstances. Initially, you may feel the need to clear your home on a daily basis, gradually reducing your clearing sessions to weekly or monthly. Listen to your intuition and you will innately know when to clear your home. If your busy schedule precludes a full clearing, you can save time by simply reciting the invocation whenever you desire.

Additionally, you can invoke The Light to maintain a sense of sacred personal space in your everyday activities, as follows:

I invoke God's Grace, which fills me, everywhere I go and everything I do, with Light. Light dissolves all Darkness, enveloping me with a Divine Barrier Shield Energy Bubble of Love, Grace, Blessings and Light:

Love, Grace, Blessings and Light to all.

While reciting the invocation, visualise your Energy Bubble extending from you outward to create a sacred personal space. Initially, recite the above invocation in full and then you can repeat a shortened version while visualising the bubble whenever you feel like an uplifting burst of The Light:

I invoke God's Grace, which fills me, everywhere I go and everything I do, with Light. Light dissolves all Darkness.

At times you may need to focus your attention on an earthly preoccupation, such as watching a film, concentrating on work or studies, engaging in a conversation or sporting activity, or at times of fatigue or recuperation, and you may be unable to consciously invoke The Light. Being the ultimate opportunist, Darkness will attempt to influence negative reactions within you or others around you in such circumstances. As a counter measure in preventing the influence of Darkness at times when your 'defences are down', simply recite the invocation once, as follows, then visualise your Companion Light Beings encircling you and transmitting The Light wherever you go and throughout all of your activities:

I invoke God's Grace, which fills me with Light. Light dissolves all Darkness, as I express my gratitude to my Companion Light Beings for continuing to transmit The Light while I am preoccupied.

Such a counter measure offers two benefits—you can enjoy your earthly preoccupation, and others can enjoy the benevolent presence of The Light! When it comes to invoking The Light or enlisting the guidance of our Companion Light Beings, we take the initiative, since our choices cannot be made for us—everything that happens in our lives results from a choice we make on some level.

Importantly, we allow The Light to do all of the work for us, leaving our will and ego out of the process entirely. Humility constitutes one of the most powerful virtues and an essential part of invoking The Light. To remove any ego influences, visualise the power and benevolence of The Light originating from God the Source of The Light, rather than from inside us (a subtle but powerful difference). Whenever invoked, The Light instantly bursts forth, channelling through our Companion Light Beings to us and radiating from us throughout the focus of our intention. Through Higher Vision, this process may appear much like the popular sculpture 'circle of friends' in symbolic form, with the person invoking The Light in the centre.

Due to the limitations of our physical bodies, our Companion Light Beings serve as Vessels of The Light, gently channelling the immense power of The Light to us whenever we invoke it and enabling us to effectively work its magic throughout all aspects of our lives. By invoking The Light, eventually we become The Light as Light Beings, effectively raising the frequency of The Light within our physical bodies and enabling us to channel the direct transmission of The Light.

MEDITATING ON THE LIGHT

Regular meditation not only offers enormous practical benefits but also a very effective way to imbibe the power and benevolence of The Light. Whether you are an experienced meditator or a beginner, this chapter will assist you in incorporating The Light into your daily meditation practice.

Choose a quiet time of day and comfortably sit cross-legged on the floor or on your meditation chair. Welcome your Companion Light Beings and express your gratitude for their benevolent guidance, support and protection. You may wish to light a candle or incense or play meditation music. In particular, the Indian musical instrument tamboura helps to effectively calm the mind.

Sit with your back straight and your palms face up on your lap, with your fingers relaxed. Breathe in and out deeply and long, three times, as follows, then breathe normally:

- On the in-breath, recite the first half of the invocation, while visualising the power and benevolence of The Light, appearing like the sun, channelling through your Companion Light Beings, immersing you, filling every cell of your being and radiating outward:

  I invoke God's Grace, which fills me with Light...

- On the out-breath, recite the second half of the invocation, while visualising any and all dark, muddy or cloudy areas within and without your auric field being cleansed by your Light-imbued breath and dissolving into the radiance of The Light within and around you:

  ...Light dissolves all Darkness.

While breathing normally, focus on the invocation by constantly reciting it for five to ten minutes, while imagining God the Source of The Light channelling rays of The Light through your Companion Light Beings, who fill and envelop your whole being with the purity of The Light, until your physical body transforms at a cellular level into The Light. See yourself as radiant, made of pure light: love and truth in its purest form. The Light awakens, refreshes and revitalises every cell of your body. A supreme being of Light, Love and Truth, you are fully aware. Meditate for a while on this sublime state.

To end your meditation session, breathe in deeply and exhale long, three times, and bring your awareness back to your physical body and your surroundings. When you feel ready, open your eyes. Take a moment to gently stretch your body and, when ready, slowly rise from your seated position.

At the end of your session, thank your Companion Light Beings for helping you to empower all of your thoughts and activities for the day with The Light by reciting:

I invoke God's Grace, which fills me, and everything I do, everywhere I go and everyone with whom I connect, with Light. Light dissolves all Darkness.

When you invoke The Light, your whole body constitutes an energy centre. You need only focus on invoking The Light, which does all the work for you in cleansing and revitalising your being, as well as releasing and dissolving any illusionary fears you may be holding. There is no need to focus on anything specific, since the all-encompassing power of The Light fills every cell of your being.

At any time, you can bring back that sublime, uplifting feeling of The Light by simply reciting the invocation. This practice will be particularly helpful should you encounter any apparent obstacles. For example, if you sense minor power struggles at work, simply invoke The Light around yourself and your colleagues and all meetings or work gatherings, and harmony will return as conflict dissipates. Make a practice of invoking The Light wherever you go, such as the supermarket, post office or gym. You will be pleasantly surprised at how smooth and effortless daily activities will become as the presence of The Light uplifts you and everyone you encounter.

Empowering Your Intentions

Although invoking The Light dissolves all fears in general, you may wish to focus your invocation on healing a particular problem area. Keep your focus positive and avoid dwelling on anything of a negative nature. Doing so empowers any fears you may be having or holding regarding the problem and may elicit a fearful rather than an uplifting response within you that may block you. Remember, Darkness is an opportunist when it comes to 'playing our chords'. Always invoke The Light whenever you sense negative feelings or thought-forms in the offing. In any case, you will be unable to empower negative intentions by invoking The Light, since doing so will negate your intention.

Adopting positive affirmations and intentions helps us to ascertain our desires. However, they may not remove all obstacles in achieving those desires or, if you do manifest your desire, you may have some difficulty around it. Regularly invoking The Light will accelerate your positive intentions, while dissolving all fears that may be blocking you. When you invoke The Light around your positive intentions, The Light does all the work for you, guiding you in the direction necessary to realise your highest desires. For example, empowering and accelerating an affirmation to attract your ideal love relationship may be recited as follows:

> *I invoke God's Grace, which fills me, and my ideal love relationship, with Light. Light dissolves all Darkness.*

Keep your invocation simple and non-specific. Additionally, you may wish to write down a detailed description to clarify your desire. Be sure to use positive terminology and describe your desire as if you have already achieved it using words such as 'I have' rather than 'I want' (which would simply reinforce a sense of lack).

Invoking The Light around your positive affirmations removes any opposition to your intentions employed by Darkness. Since you remove all expectation about how your desire may manifest, the highest outcome always results. When manifesting desires, you never have to focus on 'how', only on 'what'. When you order a pizza, you never think about how it will be made or the route the delivery man will take before arriving at your door!

The following examples illustrate the many ways you can invoke The Light to dissolve blocks, while empowering and accelerating your positive intentions and illuminating your clarity of focus:

- Invoke The Light, three times, each morning to help empower all of your daily activities and every night with the aim of enjoying a restful and rejuvenating sleep.

- When leaving your home, invoke The Light around yourself, your destination and the people with whom you will meet.

- As you get into your car, or before entering any mode of transport, invoke The Light around yourself and your transport, with the intention of filling all of your journeys with The Light, while visualising the energy of The Light expanding outward, enveloping you and your mode of transport with an Energy Bubble of The Light.

- Before initiating and while engaging in important projects, invoke The Light around yourself, the project and everyone involved.

As the following examples show, invoking The Light is flexible and can be applied in unlimited ways, as a practical everyday tool and as a powerful vehicle of enlightenment:

- Ensuring everything in your life runs smoothly and harmoniously.

- Diffusing negative or dangerous people and situations.

- Increasing motivation in a weight loss or fitness program.

- Improving health and preventing illness, since the healing energy of The Light takes place within every molecule of our being, even our DNA.

- Increasing self-confidence and your ability to create success in your life.

- Accelerating studies, career or other intellectual pursuits.

- Revealing hidden creative talents.

- Empowering a healing modality.

- Deepening a religious or spiritual practice.

- Enhancing psychic and intuitive ability.

- Becoming The Light and living life fully aware as a Light Being.

Regularly invoking The Light can empower our lives in unlimited ways.

Building Your Light Frequency

Connecting with The Light and gradually building your Light Frequency generally occurs over the following stages:

Activation:

The Activation Stage begins when you start invoking The Light and fully immerse your whole being in The Light by reciting:

I invoke God's Grace, which fills me with Light.
Light dissolves all Darkness.

During this stage you may feel as though you have to mentally and visually invoke The Light continually. Incorporating the invocation as part of a short daily meditation will help accelerate and deepen the Activation Stage. Depending on your level of commitment, this stage should last about one month.

SPRING CLEANING:

The Spring Cleaning Stage focuses on dissolving all negative influences in and around your home, at work and in all of your professional and personal relationships and activities by reciting:

I invoke God's Grace, which fills me, my home, all that I do and everywhere I go with Light. Light dissolves all Darkness.

Initially coinciding with the Activation Stage, this stage should last from three to six months, helping you to thoroughly dissolve any negative influences, until you begin imbibing The Light in everything you do.

UNCONSCIOUS INVOKING:

The Unconscious Invoking Stage enables you to invoke The Light visually around yourself and others and in all of your activities, without having to continually recite the invocation. This stage sets the foundation for embedding the practice of invoking The Light as a natural part of your life. In time, regularly invoking The Light will enable you to live life fully aware.

PART III

BEING THE LIGHT

THE LIGHT AND RELIGION

Although many of us will gravitate naturally towards The Light and welcome its inherent purity and simplicity as it resonates at the very heart of our being, the restricted belief systems of some religions may discourage a few from fully embracing a Journey of Light, even though such a journey would serve to further deepen and enhance the religious experience. In truth, all religions originate from The Light. In writing this book, I deliberately chose to communicate its messages in a very concise, more universal way. Such an approach effectively minimises the potential distractions presented by drawing associations with common religious terminology.

Originally, it was my intention to include several quotations containing 'light' as a theme as points of interest. Instead, I have included only a selection of quotations that reinforce the presence of The Light in religious belief systems. Examples of such devotional quotations include:

- "The Lord is my light, and my salvation; whom shall I fear?" (The Bible, Psalm 27:I)

- "Give light, and the darkness will disappear of itself." (Desiderius Erasmus)

- "I am the light of the world: he that followeth me shall not walk in darkness, but shall have the light of life." (Jesus Christ)

- "Let there be light!" (God the Creator)

Interpretations of some religious teachings can potentially distract us, thereby blocking The Light of Awareness. Many major religions and spiritual practices draw our focus externally, looking to an individual or deity as the focus of our enlightenment, while some maintain that the soul is inherently imperfect. Although the potential exists always for the soul to be corrupted by the illusions of the physical world, our actions or rather reactions to such illusions matter most. In the process of attaining The Light of Awareness, we destroy our ego selves, which identify only with such illusions, to uncover our true selves in The Light of our inherent divinity—our connection with God, which is neither external nor internal but all pervading.

An example of a religious teaching that may be perceived to encourage an external focus involves Jesus asking his apostles to name the Son of God. His apostles responded with several names of prophets of the time but Peter said that Jesus was the Son of God. Jesus rewarded Peter that day for his divine observation. In my opinion, Jesus lived his life in the physical world as the greatest Light Being of our age. Obviously, Jesus served as a Vessel of The Light, while other prophets simply reflected The Light, still mired in worldly illusion. Jesus offers a truly inspiring example of living life in The Light. Surely we can immerse ourselves in his teachings, while focusing on our enlightenment—a truly harmonious focus. If necessary, the invocation can be tailored easily to suit all religious beliefs.

Another example illustrating how religion may influence our perception involves Jesus saying, 'No one can come to the Father except through me'. Modern interpretations of this statement maintain that one can achieve salvation only through Jesus. Through The Light of Awareness, this teaching may be interpreted to mean 'Only through The Light can you know God'. Such an esoteric interpretation would have been difficult to understand fully. Jesus often used metaphors and parables to explain higher truths. Invoking The Light deepens our perception, enabling us to recognise the truth and meaning of divine messages.

In interpreting such religious teachings, I aim to illustrate that our enlightenment is meant to be easy. Any difficulty exists only in seeing through the Veil of Illusion and its entrapments based on the ego and fear. If Jesus lived in today's world, I am sure he would say, 'The time has come to stop emulating me and start being me'. In other words, be The Light.

Living Life Fully Aware

Eventually, the practice of regularly invoking The Light will transform you into The Light as a Light Being, enabling you to live life fully aware. Then, you will recognise Darkness before its power plays attempt to influence you. I have intuited that by 2055 we will form a society of Light Beings who will imbibe invoking The Light as a normal everyday practice and live together in sublime harmony, with fear, illness, conflict, crime and poverty conditions of the distant past.

Although everyone will attain The Light of Awareness eventually, as is our true birthright, in the meantime, Darkness will continue to exist. In a world comprised mainly of Light Beings, we will combat Darkness on a different kind of 'battle field'. Although at a much more subtle energetic level, Darkness will continue to operate using the ego as its main tool of influence. The Power Play of Darkness will no longer be able to elicit fear, since quite simply fear will not exist.

As Light Beings, we will project in and out of the physical world at will since physical death will no longer be necessary. Light Beings form their projections in the physical world quite differently. Although formulated at a much higher light/energy frequency, Light Beings will appear exactly as, and continue to coexist with, souls in physical form that have yet to attain awareness.

Attaining awareness and becoming a Light Being launches the soul's progression. In between projections, Light Beings dwell in the absolute rapture of living in the Realm of The Light. Projecting in the physical world will be considered 'a tough job but somebody has got to do it' as long as unaware souls exist. However, aside from the job of vanquishing Darkness, living life in the physical world fully aware will be virtually as rapturous.

Of course, we do not have to wait for 2055 to make a World of Light a reality. Such a joyful state can happen at any time from the moment we begin invoking The Light. In time, a regular practice of invoking The Light will transform us into Light Beings before we leave our physical projections!

Due to the high degree of Darkness in the world today, a Journey of Light at this stage in our spiritual evolution requires courage and devotion. Certainly, as more people invoke The Light, it will become easier for all of us budding Light Beings. We hardly need to teeter on the precipice of devastating conflicts or even a world war. We need only invoke The Light to change the world for the better.

PART IV

GUARDIANS OF THE LIGHT

IS YOUR LIFE PURPOSE TO PROTECT?

While visiting Santa Barbara, California, as part of the journey described in the introduction, I chose to partake in a 15-minute psychic reading. The very gifted psychic revealed that my life purpose was 'to protect'. For sometime afterwards, I pondered this revelation, wondering how it would eventually manifest in my life. Would I have to perform volunteer work at a refuge centre for the ill treated or disadvantaged? The answer came by way of a most mundane vehicle. I was drawn to see the movie *Constantine* and was stunned by how uplifted I felt. I virtually floated out of the cinema as though I was walking on clouds! The answer resonated throughout my whole being, and my true purpose became clear. I explained my revelation to a close friend, and he advised that attempting to vanquish the 'evil' of the world was not a good idea! Although appreciatively accepted, armed with stubborn determination, his warning did little to daunt my enthusiasm. About a month later, I intuited the invocation, which has evolved into the most powerful arsenal ever created to vanquish Darkness.

The Divine Life Purpose 'to protect' primarily involves channelling the power of The Light to vanquish Darkness and guide lost souls to The Light, while raising the frequency of The Light wherever you go and in all of your activities. As a Guardian of The Light, Dark Beings, particularly at a lower level, will choose to avoid you at all costs, especially as your ability to detect their presence grows, although they may haplessly cross your path from time to time. Far from the all-powerful images portrayed in films and television shows, Dark Beings only wield the illusion of power—they retreat in the presence of The Light. Additionally, people you encounter may not be aware of The Light and the influence of Darkness in their lives. Therefore, we must invoke The Light as frequently as possible. In any case, the more often we invoke The Light, the more it may benefit others and ourselves.

As a Guardian of The Light, your awareness will grow and you will recognise the following scenarios as signals alerting you to the influence of Darkness—Invoke The Light, silently, around yourself and extend The Light outward, enveloping everyone and everything involved:

- Agitated or aggressive people—Invoking The Light will diffuse any negatives or negative thought-forms promoting fearful reactions.

- Conflicts as a result of arguments or intimidating behaviour—When you invoke The Light, conflict dissipates and harmony abides.

- Sounds of alarms or police and ambulance sirens—Invoke The Light around your neighbourhood, as well as the source of the sound and everyone involved.

- Scenes of accidents or tragic events, even those you see on newscasts—You can invoke The Light from any distance.

- Warfare between people and nations—Invoking The Light calls forth immense power, transforming the greatest soldier into the mightiest advocate of peace.

As these examples illustrate, Darkness influences fearful reactions in so many ways. In such instances, you may feel drawn to 'do battle' to rid the world of Darkness. To resolve the battle, simply invoke The Light. In a short time, you will become a truly formidable Guardian of The Light!

CONCLUSION

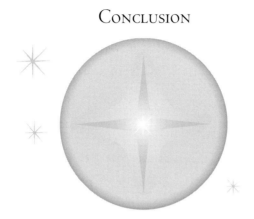

G ood intentions keep the world together. Many well-intentioned people do great things through philanthropy, charitable causes and great personal self-sacrifice; but they are constantly frustrated and blocked by the antics of Darkness, ranging from petty annoyances to major roadblocks, even untimely death, if left unchecked. Others simply remain unconvinced, living life 'on the fence'.

Often we hear people say, 'How can God allow bad things to happen to good people?' If it is true that everything happens according to a Divine

Strategic Plan, within which we may instil our choices and set paths influenced by The Light or Darkness, then we must ASK OURSELVES this question. We are free to choose the paths we follow. 'Will' only exists through us. God the Source of The Light never imposes will. The Light frees us, while Darkness enslaves us. Life in the physical world challenges us to destroy the ego or be destroyed by the ego. Darkness maintains that by destroying the ego and embracing The Light, we lose ourselves. This belief is erroneous; by embracing The Light we lift the Veil of Illusion only to find ourselves.

Without The Light to guide and protect us, we must contend with the Power Play of Darkness, driven by the relentless aim of Darkness to douse The Light of Awareness.

Many examples illustrate this point, including:

- participants of self-development seminars who walk away on a high note, feeling a great sense of optimism with renewed personal goals, only to be disappointed and fall back into self-sabotage the moment a negative experience surfaces; or

- philanthropists who perform great selfless acts, while struggling with deeply-troubled personal lives, only to end up, at best, ostracised by the very communities they love and serve or, at worst, having their lives end tragically.

These examples represent good people with good intentions at two very wide ends of the scale. Nonetheless, Darkness influences everyone, regardless of their intentions—unless they invoke The Light. The life of the late Mother Teresa presents another good example to illustrate this point. Like all saints, unconsciously, she refused to 'sell out' to Darkness and ended up paying a high personal price by choosing to live in abject poverty, while completely rejecting the material world. Some people may feel they have to give in to Darkness to succeed; after all it seems to rule the world!

In truth, we do not have to give up our possessions to find ourselves, nor must we give in to Darkness to live a life of luxury and success. I passionately believe we deserve the best in our lives. Additionally, God the Source of The Light wishes the best for us always. Conversely, Darkness employs its power plays through an insidious cocktail of the ego and the illusion of power, fuelled by fear, with which to work through or 'play' us. Fear exists only if we 'buy into it'. Invoking The Light renders fear, exercised through the Power Play of Darkness, powerless.

Invoking The Light is the most powerful way to remove Darkness from your life and the lives of those you love, as well as your community and the world at large. If enough people invoke The Light on a worldwide scale, we can transform the world until it truly becomes Heaven on Earth.